ECHOES OF SILENCE

A SECOND COLLECTION OF POEMS AND SHORT STORIES

ECHOES OF SILENCE

A Second Collection of Poems and Short Stories

David Crossan-Bratt

TAKAHE PUBLISHING LTD.

2019

This edition published 2019 by:
Takahe Publishing Ltd.
Registered Office:
77 Earlsdon Street, Coventry CV5 6EL

Dedicated to the memory of

John and Mary Crossan-Bratt

(who would have never believed that I would do this)

and

to all my carers who made this possible

Acknowledgements

The author would like to thank all the kind readers who encouraged him to write a second book.

To a particular friend who commented that she didn't know what I had for a brain, but evil dark worms must crawl through it.

A special thanks to my publisher for all his hard work.

CONTENTS

Poems

Short Stories

"Those cries ripped through the present of that time and revealed another dimension.

A kind of potent demonstration, absurd perhaps, perhaps without purpose, but we attempt not to forsake and not to lose …… the devotion to these values which only the flames could put an end to."

Landscapes of the Metropolis of Death

Otto Duv Kulka

"The mad thought he had been supported by death and nothingness ….. This dreaming return to a ruling function of nothingness"

Palace of the Peacock

Wilson Harris

The Hermit

By choice
It's a cold house I live in

No fires
    give heat here. Even in
    winter's heart there is no form of heating
    and I freeze into myself for warmth
Drawing on an inner flame to burn
off all accretions.
This is no punishment or penance
but a deliberate approach for

    Purity.

Uncluttered,

    Unattached,

    Unspoiled,

Completely alone and unadorned, forced
out of this life by

    the rigour of the regime

and disciplined with the strength of stone.

Summary Evening Song

Now that the heat is gone
The long slow sunset turns to
twilight, violet and golden, and
Within the crepuscular stillness
The swifts swoop and stir
the evening sky,
Undramatically dusk descends and deepens,
A pale green moon rises above the river

While I reach for your hand
Feeling only the emptiness,
The moon turns pale and punches a
hole in the sky for darkness to pour through
All that is left is space and the silence
Open and endlessly resonating with your
Memory in every sound under the stars
Indistinct, distant, desolation and despair
Reverberating in the half dead whispers of the night

16/9/08

Song for Someone Special

I kept myself cavey baby, did not dare to admit
That I could care about you or the things that you did
But as the days go on and with each new dawn
I find myself forgetting, I cannot forget

      Your pale grey eyes and
      The sound of your voice
      And I am lost in reverie and need to rejoice

For you are someone special baby, you need to understand
That all of your problems come from your own hand
Not knowing what is good for you, or what will make you smile
I find myself thinking of you all the while

      Your pale grey eyes and
      The sound of your voice
      And I am lost in reverie and need to rejoice

You don't know what you mean to me baby and I don't
    suppose you care
It seems your life has the lightness of swallows taking to the air
But I have seen your darkness baby and know the depths of
    your despair
Will only come to an end and when you let a friend
Unlock your sorrows and you start to rejoice
At the sound of your own voice
So brighten your eyes, and let us comprise
A life that's given meaning to by simply being you
As your pale grey eyes and the sound of your voice
Leaves me in reverie baby and helps me rejoice

Psalm 1

to Stephanie

"Teach us to care, and not to care" - T.S. Eliot

With your languid air of slothfulness
and louche approach to life
You enchanted me with your ability to care
And deal with all the vicissitudes of mind
With a sneering smile or stare
Or word expressing do not dare
Stretch familiarity too deep or practise études
Too long, or try to expose the essential truths
That lie:
This precocious countenance, as the lion lies down
with the lamb
Giving love to all these strangers,
Who search for your heart and soul
Greatly aware of all the dangers
And the feelings you must control
Caring and not caring so you can gain the crown
So hardly won and richly earned
As on each soul your power has burned.

fide et amore

Fellow Traveller of the Night

Fellow traveller of the night
Whoever you are or were or wished to be
Now with your dreams crossed
And a burning soul of white fire
Walking through the wakeful midnight
Through these dirty city streets
Gouged out of concrete
Grimmed with age
To where the oily waters sleep
I'm the one who travels with you

Like a silver dagger of remorse
The moon upon your back
Far closer than your shadow
I'm the one in steady tread of your step
That sends you forward never faltering
Through the blanket night or the blackest path
Leaving behind the lilting laughter and
The joyous light
Which left us uneasy in its ease
My brother-soul, my fellow traveller of the night

Preparing for Winter

Now the mornings dawn grey and we can't hope
to see sun before ten.
If I bothered to check there is probably rime round the pool
and the brittle grass still bears footprints
from the invisible animals of night.
There is an easy calm around the house
like in the room of one dying of old age
or a long illness;
No pain or sorrow just the slumberous
breathing of the house laying
to rest.

Is it just imagination? Do the
bones in the footings stir and turn, just
once, in recognition of the autumn
equinox?

The mouse in the rafters
starts in, scurries pink eyed and alert,
tugging a loose piece of grain.
The earth moves in its bed as a
leaf sinks into the soil
And the church bell tells another assumption.
First flames flicker in the hearth
as the cat turns and settles;
preparing for winter.

Slope End September 79

The Poet at the Point of Desperation

It is a lonely world inside a poem

Words whirl and wave,
      always out of
              reach
let me put on my antic disposition

and run Learlike headlong into the storm
smashed sentences blown bricks on the brain.

      Let me garb myself in the garbled grammar
of centuries
      half learned and now unable to comprehend
the age
      or tie down to the page
      for study by some famous sage

Now half dead or not living at all

      And having applied the ink to the paper
in these long scrolling lines
      Let them lie there treacherous in their unthreatening
      attitude

      So he went away again.

Distraction

(to Lynn, now dead)

It's that time of day when I can never work
When consciousness becomes a seagull
darting at distraction, lemmings in a silver sea,
more important than the words I pursue across the page.
The autumn sun through the library window induces sleep
as slowly the eyes stop focusing.

Then there is you in another time
The sun is warm on our bodies, nearly naked.
It seems so long ago, and it is,
a spent moment is eternity away and can never be redeemed
we are not consubstantial with our past which is merely
a definition of hopes fulfilled or forgotten or killed.
Now it inhabits our memories but has no existence,
like you in another time
a memory without existence that can never be redeemed
and which I can never follow.

And when I rise on the next wave of consciousness
I find you fled further in the past.

21/10/79

8

The Glorious Dead

The shadows of ghosts inhabit my dreams
tenebrael whispers in the twilight of the soul
Pursued by phantoms, inaudible breathing
These whitewashed silent walls scream out
with shell song whistling in the air and exploding in the head
Tramping over another twisted body melting in the mud
All life blown open and squashed out
Sacrificed for glory
And still they come the lost legions
Over the top and into the mud
Blood, viscera, and the stinking slime and excremental remains
of regiments
Resigned to slaughter

Somewhere beside me, an explosion
Some are gone, some remain, warm and wet on my face and
hands
Sticking to my clothing and boots
Dragging me down to drown in their slough and slurry
I long to sink into the earth
Real men would have laid down screaming
But we were the already dead
And so we walked on
Our minds numb, eyes open but sightless in the smoke
And ears blasted silent by the noise

You never thinking, brought me here
To see a monument in memory of the fallen
An object of civic pride
To honour the dead
The lucky dead, remembered with walls of whitewash and lies
Built with blood money, blackmailed on grief
Having sacrificed their sons
A monument built by public subscription

"It's for our Harry and Stevie, and all the other boys," she says
with pride and tears
On a city growing fat on War bonds and military ordinance
orders
Each named tree nurtured forever if a family could afford so
many shillings of silver
He died anonymously
There was no name on the shell that killed him, alongside so
many others
Unknown in mist, mingling in the muck and unity with his pals

These walls have eyes, ever staring, never seeing
Eyes fixed and hard, eyes speaking
That strange, soundless accusation of anger and pain
These eyes of sorrow staring at a card
Thanking you for your loved one
Who died with valour?
Fighting for his King and Country
Did he Hell! All bloody lies
He died under the wheels of an ammunition cart
Carrying Coventry's shells for boys back behind the lines
Slipped in the mud and got run over
Squealed like a pig, he did.
And screamed and screamed
Screamed louder than the shells around us
As the column moved on
The iron wheels rolling unable to stop
We were being shelled, could've blown the bloody lot!

His eyes beseeching help and the voice quietened
As his mouth filled with mud
Still light in his eyes begging for help, imploring help

Now growing dimmer, then condemning us all
For living, his only relief was death
Death slow

Death not glorious
Death drowned in mud
The eyes gone cold
Staring and calling out till the end
Eyes condemning the living
Just eyes that I can't forget
Eyes that haunt me and taunt me with cowardice
But I had no choice
The column moved on
The eyes didn't, but they return everywhere
There is no glorious death

Night Thoughts

Watching Hesperus and Vaudeville between
Main Street and the Bridge
Two broken hearted lovers playing spin
the bottle for the cops
and wait to see which way the shilling falls to decide
who goes on top for there
ain't no heroic actions when the rituals are real
while the Chinese croupier arranges another deal and
ambitions choke with cigarette smoke and the stairs
are stained with puke.
The dog rose worries at the trellis of a
garden overgrown and rank
Where weeds prickle like the truth but it doesn't matter
at the time
as she undoes another button on her too cheap
evening dress and arranges how she's sitting
to reveal her blue veined breasts
The stage is like a catafalque on which
the dead can act
Under the smoke stained ceiling of some electric night
but the cops ain't asking questions they have
seen the burned contract
and someone gave the lovers a blood stained Bowie knife
To cut the heart out of each other for
a simple act of faith and greed
so we smile and plead our innocence and try
to leave without a trace forgetting that everything
is paid for by the lines upon our face
But the ever smiling bouncer and the cop don't seem too
    concerned
as we pass the booth where Hesperus and Vaudeville
share out what they've earned.

Psalm 2

to Daniela

I am a poet out of time
Looking for words that rhyme
And struggling to speak truth
To your grace, and proof
of your simple soulfulness,

Moving with quiet elegance
Affirming an angelic presence
While silently shouldering situations without stress,
A comforting servant to strangers
And testament that all the changes

Are illusion and lies as we seek
Our shared humanities, and peace
Transcending earthly understanding
As our individuality is disbanding

Swan Song

Then the lady went off with a gipsy
and the circus boys beneath
The crying clowns and the baying hounds
and the dancers' snarling teeth
created commotion on the highway
with an over- elaborate plea for
one crushed by circumstances and
a woman beyond belief
who nobody can rely on

Butterflies and diamonds are falling on the street
small green eyes accuse of lies the
man who wants to rage against the
tide of time and the hopeless rhyme
in a rhythm out of beat

The dawn waits for a hanging with a slowly
creeping sweep
of a shadow across a courtyard on which the
rain competes
with the cry of one too numb
to weep but to suddenly reappear seared
by the air and the last light
soon to open beneath his feet

14

Responsibility

I would spit in the face of
God for you
And take a risk on eternity

You are part of all my waking hours
and the end of all reason
To betray you now that
times are tough
Would be the greatest treason
Yet if I really love you
I must accept your freedom

And leave you to discover
who is truly you
Hoping you love her as I do
So you may return to me
and take me as your lover
facing life's ultimate absurdity

Lies

Your last smile you gave with little grace
More a sign of sadness as it left your face
But I accepted it with trust and said farewell
Not realising the lies a smile can tell

Darkness Opens

To open a new life and find a new world
This is what is offered
in the dark night in which you embark

The old dispensation grows tired
and it is time to leave
freedom allows only choice
So you must grasp the moment
As time's vortex claims you
Hurling you into eternity, unable
to heed the meaning of the endless

Blow winds, howl and rage
Blood will have its day, smash the facade
of reason and respectability
Accepts the emptiness which is all the answers
to questions no longer asked
You are the question and the answer
Crushing against the wall of history
But loosening it, dissolving it in a deep
lacuna of darkness in which
all action is its own explanation
and all explanation is invalid

Counterfeit

She counted the flowers
    I numbered the clouds
She worked in hours
    I worked in crowds

She collected memories
    I collected faces
She asked for testimonies
    I lost the traces

Now somewhere among the clouds
    I search for her memory
Alone among the crowds
    Living with sweet anomie

Memories and Mist

As we come to the end of the day,
Sunset and evening star, a sickle
Moon swathed in sea mist rises
Across the bay, so near and yet
So far, you are a presence impossible
To forget, or to quite remember

Tired waves whisper against the strand
Each carrying a quiet cadence of
Distance and regret where I stand
In this emptiness of time and space
Staring at the mist, imagining
Images of your face forming into
A memory of haze and past times
Recalling a lost embrace, for
I am lost, lost without will,
Without choice, I loved you then
And yet I love you still

October 2018

Above Mount Grace Priory

The winter sky
　　Grey and vast from Pennine to the coast
The air still as death and the
　　ground hard as the question of eternity
standing stone still unable to break the spell
　　of light and cloud and distance
Immersed in emptiness
　　till somewhere a curlew shrieks and splits the
Moment from the place
　　forcing everything back into time
And the silent cars stream
　　up and down the distant highway
a world away

The Price

She looked beautiful in her mourning dress
Proud and determined not to weep
Two children trail behind the folds of her coat
Confused and frightened by all
The flashlights and strangers
Her moment of fame had arrived
Uninvited and at such a price

Remembrance Day 2018

The Haunting

It's an old feeling of dark and thunder,
of night winds blowing cold
An old feeling of hopeless wonder
of a lost and lonely child

Now the past is my only present
and my mind is full of memories
in this all too quiet house
My head swims with wild contents
like ululating ancient threnodies
repeated across the endless hours

It's the old feeling of mist and mountains
of cobwebs growing grey
But still the memories remain
to haunt me every day

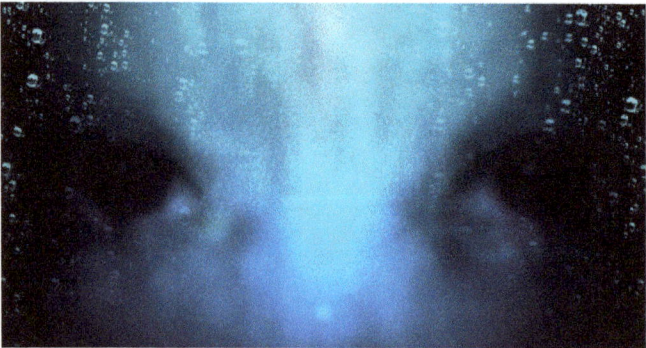

Winter Sparrows

A dry leaf is blown across the lawn
Dark dots appear on the bare branched
Winter trees, twittering small notes
On the stave of the dawn , they
Flutter and balance in the air
Leading to a melody that takes off
In many directions, but bringing
Some light to a grey morning

And somewhere, in the distance,
High, high up in the air,
Not music but the memory of music
Now echoed, and re-echoed in the wind
So the dry leaves quiver on the branch
As the sparrows return, a promise
Of music on a dull day

History

To open a new life, to find a new world,
This is what is offered
in the dark night in which you embark

This old dispensation grows tired
and it is time to leave
freedom dictates choice, and this is ours constantly
So grasp the moment,
the vortex claims you as its own
Enter it filled with wonder
Be hurled into eternity unheeding of any fears
and grasp the meaning of eternity
crushing it to your will

Scream winds and smash against all form
Blood will have its day, rage against
the facade of reason and respectability
accept the emptiness which is all the answers,
the questions are no longer asked

You are the questions and the answers
Crashing against the wall of history
But bending it, dissolving it as the imposter It is,

A lacuna in which all
action forms its own explanation
and all explanation is invalidated as
We return to our beginning

Existence

One aircraft many miles away
Cuts a white streak
Across a pale blue sky
Between the cliffs of clouds
And without any noise it is gone

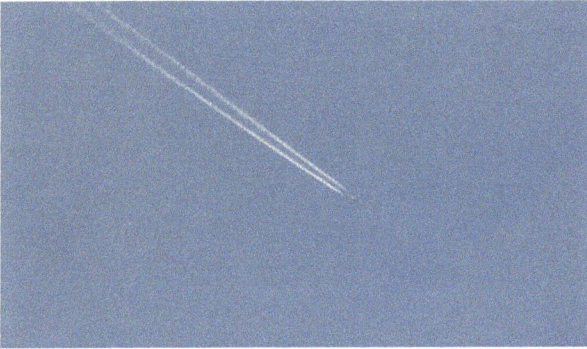

Memory and Change

In these dead hours, the
cold dawn of life and waking dreams
waiting for the wind to change

In the still air no bird sings
the sun is a blind eye's stare
smothered by a grey sky

All hope is burnt away by
the soft wind blowing across barren cliffs

Yet something stirs in my memory
I remember your lion's hair and haughty grandeur
were only belied by your empty laughter
and your eyes melting to tears

Then I wish I could make you smile
and now you say all right let us try

Within this wilderness of our creation
To overcome this loveless isolation

The Question

Above the fields
An apology for the moon hangs
isolated in the November sky
Like a half finished question mark
Asking where has my bold pride gone and
Who are these pale shadows
rising all around, insubstantial and numberless
As the stars that begin to shine
in the deepening darkness
And the only answer is silence and tears

11 November 2018

Song for September

I didn't see you to the door
or take you by the hand
or see any sense in kissing you
but as you move across the floor
leaving only emptiness and sand
there's a deep feeling of missing you

The years so quickly past
are fading into grey
leaving just a photograph

There's no longer any future
to plan or play for
as all my schemes come crumbling
I am lost in a culture
I'm going to have to pay for
As my guilty dreams come tumbling

Its the old feeling of mountains and mist
of loss both real and fey
the feelings in my heart persist
as you are going away

Dog End Days

Now is the world grown small
Sealed in upon itself
The sky sits on my shoulder
And I walk in cold clouds of drenching non-rain
All colour is drained out of life
leaving only grey streets
of grey houses, grey lights and grey noise
Grey cars approach, two hopeless
headlights looming in isolation
Fighting against the sunless half-light

A Gogmagogic giant moves effortlessly
through the gloom
Revived from prehistory by this miasma
Is revealed as a pitiful solitary
man wrapped up in separation
underneath a cap and driven deep
into an overcoat by the oppressive elements

The silence hangs heavy with foreboding
As breath streams into the dark air
like the spirit leaving the body of the dead
Bent stiff figures shuffle past unspeaking
All communication suspended
and senseless sound suppressed
The dogs have ceased barking
and even Cerebus lies silent,
No birds sing

And every individual invents an
interior language to convey the
Mournful melancholy of these
Dog end December days
Dragging down to the solstice

The Lady of the Dawn

You blinded me with your beauty
As we danced beneath the stars,
I courted you in my dreams
I courted you in bars

I thought you were the answer
But you became another cause
And now it seems our passion
Has the cold fire of wars

While you have left me homeless,
Stripped naked, without a friend
Yet as you put me to the test
With whom should I contend?

For there are no furling banners
Or trumpets on the wind
As I walk with head bowed down
Wearing the ashes of one who's sinned

For all the women of Lebanon
And all the women of the street
Regard me with eyes of cool
Knowing I could not compete

For your beauty left me startled
As we danced towards the dawn
Little did I realise
How soon I'd find you gone

Dark Night

Out here the stars are bright
The ancient constellations
Not muffled by the city lights
But that is no consolation
I'd come back tomorrow
If I thought that you'd be waiting

But my love is a dream
A shooting star that's fading
Yet I'm constant as the Northern Star
Left lonely, isolated and freezing
Yet no astrologer can map
Out the reasons for you leaving

Now I am standing silent
Beneath a sky of sorrow
Watching the shimmering stars
That will die before tomorrow
As I recall the emptiness in your eyes
And the coldness of our goodbyes

Wondering where you are
I question where am I
For nothing bites like loneliness
In the monotony of night
When darkness seems endless
As you have stolen all the light

Echoes of Silence

The voice of God was not in the whirlwind
Silence is a voice exploding in the mind –
Shell-shock – the remorseless resonance of the nothing that is.
Is it that expression of compassion that speaks
only to the eye, the empathy instantly felt, instinctively
    understood.
Or the iteration of contemptibility, the silent
smack in the face of a shrug that smarts
in the mind for months

In your heart can you hear a still small
voice that makes for righteousness,
but that you are not sure you hear aright.
It is more like a Chinese whisper or a wish
fulfilment sent to test our certainty

I have no conviction or certainty.

Spring Tees

*April come she will when streams are ripe
and swelled with rain*
                                    Paul Simon

As the snow retreats on the distant hills
The river runs brown and rich in sedimentary
remains, dragged from the upland peats, ferns and mosses.
Multicolour soup seeps through moor grass and heather
root and fills the springlets and drainage ditches, and
the rills of dark water rushing from the
headlands to restore the rivers flow and carry the
nutrients to awaken sullen Spring to the call
from the hills that loom a blue grey mass on the horizon.

The season requires renewal and procreation swells all
along the river and in response yellow squeaking balls of
ducklings wallow at the shallow water's edge, marshalled
by a mother to keep them from being swept away by the
        current.
She senses danger and soon they are hidden in the new
grown river grass swaying in the breeze.

A gust of South West wind promises rain.
Swiftly the sky turns slatelike, featureless and on which
        nothing
is written unless concealed in the river's moving mirror,
and carried in the lapping ripples along the banks wordless
whispers of unknown futures.

As thick black clouds lumber over the distant hills,
a daydream of night engaging headlight, street
lights and houselights that fall in crazy patterns
on the river. A modern mobile work of art – The river
Abstract, plastic, unable to be held but fleetingly real.

Soon the first rain falls, slow heavy drops exploding on
impact, indiscriminate but bearable, no need to
shelter, but soon rain falls fierce and fast in straight
lines that splinter and spot on tiles and tin roofs, and
the river boils with indignation as arrow straight
the rain strikes to its very heart.

Sitting on the soft sand beneath a bridge
all around is dusk at noon and a grey haze.
As water strikes water and the far river bank is lost
    In spray.

    This is the river's Spring.

Nothing Moved

a short story

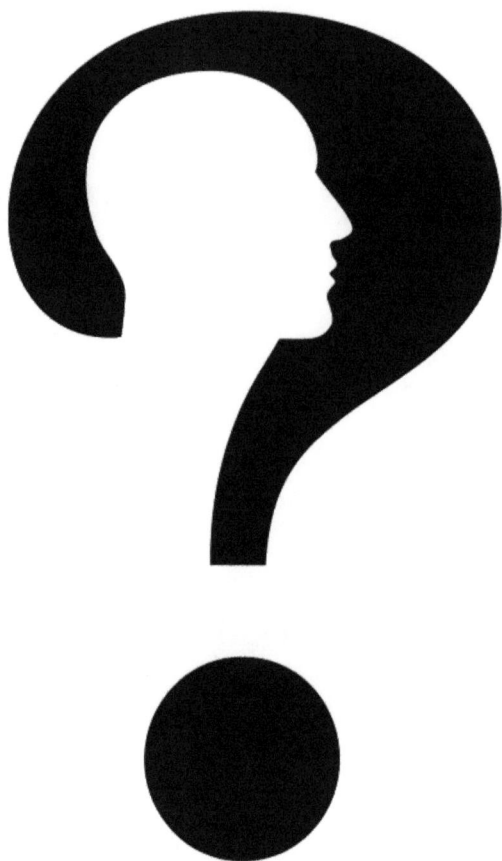

NOTHING MOVED

As soon as he awoke he knew it was not right. The bed felt strange, it was firm but not hard as he expected to find his bed. Even before he moved, things were out of place. There was something alien about the darkness that told him this was not his room. It felt closed in, confining and intimidating. There was an unwelcome intimacy about the blackness that made him uneasy, although he could not have said why. It seemed to know him, to envelope him and interrogate him just by its emptiness, but at the same time it was close and oppressive.

He made his first conscious decision of the day. He would expel the darkness and bring everything back into order. Reaching up, he searched for the light switch behind his bed. With increasingly rapid sweeps, his hand sought out salvation from the searing darkness. With some alarm, he realised this was not his bed, not his room. He lay still and tried to figure out how he had got here. Could he remember the previous evening, had he been drunk, had somebody taken pity on him and given him a bed for the night? There were no answers. Whatever he had done was completely wiped out. This did not worry him, he was quite used to a form of drunken amnesia, at times he even played a little game with himself seeing how long it would take before he would recall an event. Some, of course, never came back. He decided just to let time take its course. But then he could not recall any cause for getting drunk, or drinking, or companions in drink. And his body did not feel as though he had been drinking. There were no aches or muscular pains, no dry mouth, no nausea, in fact none of the usual punishments for enjoying life too much.

He realised that he was now playing a game with himself and remembered a name, the name of a book "Homo Ludens". He is a games player and here he was trying to work out the rules to solve the puzzle. If he were to wake up in a totally dark room with no memory of how he got there, what would he do next?

Why do anything? Probably it would be best to lie here and wait for somebody to come and explain how everything had happened. Why should he struggle when they would fill in the blanks. He thought that would have been fine if he had a hangover; in fact to be left to live quietly would of been a blessing. Being clearer headed as he was, lying here was a zero option. It appeared too passive and lacking in vitality.

There were voices. Somewhere, a long way off, people were talking in muffled incoherent speech that rolled through the dark, and footsteps, heavy like distant thunder. They pounded away in the background and sounded like boots on an uncarpeted floor. Had he been arrested, was he in some police cell?, he wondered. But again, he had no memory of being in any trouble.

Without warning he was chided by a harsh white light that filled his head and left no space for understanding. Gradually the room came into focus and the blazing light moved from behind his eyes back into the room, flooding it with a fluorescent glare. His eyes started to discern shapes that quickly become solid and formed themselves into the usual furnishings of a bedroom – a wardrobe, a small table and a sink. He let his eyes drift from object to object making it real by absorbing its colours and its substantialbility. On one wall were a pair of brightly printed curtains and almost opposite there was the door, a pale white colour nothing unusual. As he became more accustomed to the light, he noticed there was a key in the door and for some reason this reassured him. At least, he felt, he could not have been locked up.

He felt a tremendous urge to get up and try the door, to see what was outside and if it gave any clues to his present position. But almost as soon as this thought crossed his mind, it was countered by a desire to snuggle further down under the bedclothes and to enjoy the security and warmth they provided and he found himself pulling the blankets up over his head to shut out the artificial light. He felt strangely threatened by its brash harshness. The bed had already become familiar, and a place of safety.

He did not know how long he stayed like this or even if he went back to sleep. Nor could he remember any conscious thought or any dreams, but when he next looked around the blankets, the room was exactly the same. A screaming light that came from nowhere and penetrated everywhere allowing no shadows.

The furniture was all arranged in the same places that he remembered them. The room was becoming familiar and although not friendly, it did offer some sense of being and belonging. He knew that he must get out of bed and explore the room and make it his.

After a few more minutes hesitation, he flung back the bed covers and dived off the bed as he used to do on winter mornings of his childhood before central heating; bedrooms were always cold and frost would pattern the window-panes. To his surprise he was fully dressed. It was something he had not even considered while in bed but now here he stood in full suit and tie, all the way down to a pair of carefully polished brown shoes. He looked for a mirror to inspect himself, but there was none.

He went to the wardrobe to see if there were any other clothes that could give him a clue about himself or his whereabouts but it was empty and anonymous. He went to the sink and to his relief he found that the taps worked. Turning both full on he washed his face and eyes and wet his neck. He looked up to see his face in the mirror he expected to be above the sink, but it was not there, only a blank wall. Moving to the curtains he thought to draw them back in the hope of being able to see himself in the window glass and at least get some idea of his general position. Was he in the country or a town, what was the weather like, could he see anything around him that would give a clue to his position? As the curtains were withdrawn his heartbeat rose as his uncertainty increased and he felt himself becoming more confused. Behind the curtain was just another blank wall. This was getting beyond a joke, whatever was happening to him and whoever was doing it was starting to go too far. He wanted an explanation and he wanted it now. Angrily he moved to the door and tried to pull it open but it was stuck or locked. He looked at the key, huge and old. It was really too big for a bedroom door. He tried to turn it and expected to hear some movement in the mechanism, but it merely turned through the full circle. He tried it again and again, in exasperation pulling and pushing the door but nothing moved. He tried banging on the door and shouting but to no avail, clearly nobody was concerned about him.

He tried to think what he should do next. What did people want of him; was he being watched? He felt the cold sweat on the base of his spine and realised that he was about to start to panic. The knowledge in itself caused him to stop, he clenched his fists and felt his nails bite into his fleshy palms. His head was clearing, obviously someone had placed him here, if they wanted to see him break they could wait. He looked around for a lens but nothing was obvious. There was no-one to stick a finger up to; no-one to challenge or defy.

By now he was calm, he was determined to grasp back whatever control he could in this unequal situation. If there was nothing he could do, he would choose to do nothing. He would go back to bed and wait for his captors to reveal themselves. His inactivity would force them to show themselves, and make them enter into dialogue with him. He had read somewhere that this was the way to deal with kidnappers and terrorists. He must get them to talk, get them to admit your humanity and try and build up a relationship with whoever had placed him here. When you knew who you were dealing with you could start to develop plans.

There was no need to do anything if you did not even know the agenda. Everything you planned could be totally wrong if you had targeted the wrong adversary as they obviously had already done. For why should they have taken you, you had no influence, no position, no value as a bargaining token. Nobody cared about you. You were not important, as far as you knew. You could have been a teacher, a drifter and one of those people who wandered from hot-spot to hot-spot just to watch the drama unfold. Nobody paid you for being there and nobody was responsible for getting you out of any situation into which you fell. He returned to bed and decided to sleep. Then he questioned why he thought he had been kidnapped. Could it just be that a jealous husband had decided to teach him a lesson. He looked at his body under the bed clothes. Although well dressed it did not look like the body of a philanderer. He remembered times when he would have tried to take on any female challenge but the body he was wearing was too old and anyway his mind was not working like that. He really did not feel that he was a sexual being capable of causing this kind of revenge. His mind went into overload, was it an old girl-friend determined to exact her ultimate punishment for some former slight? Had she organised his capture and was about to take out her anger and frustration on him? Looking down the bed it seemed unlikely. That sort of thing did not really happen, not in real life. It was the stuff of those top-shelf magazines, written by bored soldiers in dodgy barracks half a world away.

Before he got any more farcical ideas, he decided to will himself to sleep. The bed now felt as though it fitted him and he curled up under the warmth of the blankets. He could not tell whether he had slept or not. He was aware that there had been long periods of silence but how long? He lay and concentrated on the silence. Was there anything behind the silence, anything inside that irritating and compelling emptiness? He knew now that he must not let himself slip away again. His only grasp of reality was if he chose every moment. The decision to sleep or not sleep must be taken as a full conscious result of addressing all the other possibilities. It would be better to sleep when he did not feel tired so that he could monitor his body and censor his dreams. Obviously all obsessive ideas, all outside influences must be filtered to prevent whoever had trapped him here gaining some control of his mind. But as he thought this, he immediately wondered whether his mind had already gone; was he getting paranoiac about a broken door-lock?

He decided to close his eyes. He decided to let images and dreams happen so that when he remembered them he could analyse their significance and make the whole story out of all these fragments. It was becoming very dark and he wondered if those wounding bright lights had gone out but chose not to check. The sky flashed behind his eyelids, bright white, and grey, and orange flashes lit the firmament behind his sealed eyelids. And from the back of the celestial light show, high grey figures lumbered between the shooting stars and the lightning. They stomped centre stage and gradually revealed themselves. Initially they were just giant grey grotesques from some Spanish carnival. Some were immediately recognisable as friends from a previous age, others took longer to bring back to consciousness. They were becoming more substantial, colour was returning to their forms; the grey grotesques were becoming personalities, people he knew. Some he loved, some he hated, many were just people he met occasionally but he could not explain what they were doing in this room or in his head, whichever was most solid.

He heard a clock strike six times. Was it morning or was it evening? And then only a few minutes later he heard another clock. This time it was closer, time was coming towards him. He heard it moving in six simple beats. Time was approaching and then was struck six times, then another clock only slightly further away. He followed it, as somewhere high above, a majestic chime rang out.

The chiming of six o'clock across an unseen landscape, each church or civic centre recording the hour as it reached them and so six o'clock went and on and on across the globe leaving him behind. Was it six o'clock? And if so what did it mean? When did the cock crow on Peter and did it matter? He had betrayed nobody. He had nobody to betray.

For the first time, he became aware that he had no knowledge of day and night. He did not know how long the lights were on or off. Nobody had been to see him. At times he rattled the door or watched just to see if it was still there. Most of the time he spent crawled under his blanket. There were periods of absolute silence. He had begun to like these but suddenly they would be pierced by the most heart-rending cries as though young babies were being thrown into fires, or beasts burnt alive. Yet when it all subsided, there would be knocking on his door, but nobody ever came in. He would lie under his blanket shivering not daring to speak or go to the door and eventually the noise would stop. After the screams and the knocking there was often a period of peace and quiet.

It was during one of these respite times that he became aware of a crackling noise. It was very different to the other disturbances that he felt around here. Soon he felt hot, the temperature in the room was rising quickly and soon grey and white smoke was coming under the door and through all the cracks in the woodwork. The building was obviously on fire, but no-one had come to save him. There were no fire alarms or sounds of urgency. Could the building have been deliberately set ablaze with him inside?

He could not understand what he had done just to be left. Had he been abandoned or simply forgotten? Or was this the end planned for him? Was he going to die without explanation of why he was here, who had brought him or what they had wished to gain? There were no explanations. Perhaps there never had been. Perhaps all his wonderings had been only to prepare him for this. To prepare him for the utter impossibility of meaning and the imponderability of living.

His mind was besieged both by panic and by questions "Why?" Why me, why not? What have I done, what do they want? Have they got the wrong person? The whole ceiling was now alight. Purple and pink flames skipped across the roof tiles as they started to melt and fill the room with dripping flames and black smoke.

It was suddenly the only hope. With luck the whole ceiling and roof may fall in before this inferno devours me, he thought. This gave him the ability to soar to freedom through the roof space and rejoin the stars. Cold blue fire in the bubble of eternity as he expanded into the void. Then he knew he was free and had never been captive.

The Chairman

a short story

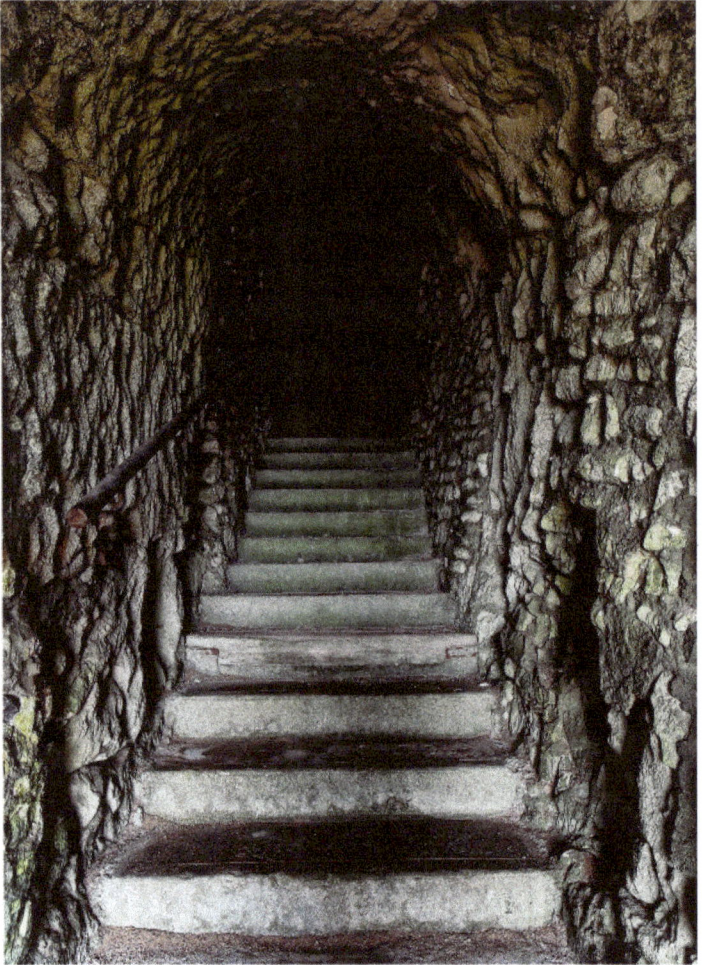

THE CHAIRMAN

The focal point of the room would have been the fireplace if only the fire had been lit. But it was not and had not been for a long time. Now it remained a vast, blank space, empty and bare like the gaps between the stars. Of course, there were no stars, only a lacuna in the unremarkable wall of the cold room, where the dust seemed to be the only thing that would move. But it did not move.

In the quiet of the room the noise of heavy breathing threatened to disturb the dust. Rhythmic, measured breaths, exhaled with long spaces between. "Aagh", he growled from the depth of his high padded seat in which a man of his bulk could not get comfortable, but he never thought of changing his chair. "Aagh", he repeated. The guttural sound of saliva and mucus rattled round his throat.

"Do you want something, sir?" said a voice from a shadowy corner at the far end of the room from the seated personage. The end from which you would enter whenever you were unfortunate enough to have reason to call at this room.

"If I wanted something, I would have asked. Shut up". The last command was hardly necessary as the other one had already settled himself back in the silence. The one on the chair shifted his bulk slightly on to the other buttock and then the room fell again into its mausoleum-like silence.

Half an hour passed. The grey day settled into dull evening as the light began to fail. The sound of rain could be heard hammering but very gently, almost reverently, it seemed, on the small square window panes.

"It's getting dark, let there be light", he said. Immediately, but softly, matches could be heard scratching and two sets of feet, in carpet slippers, shuffled round the great empty room and lit seven menorahs. These were placed just so the light from each arc intersected that of the arc next to it and the shadows between them intertwined in a slow dance which betrayed some movement of air in the still room.

Suddenly: "Have you anything to say, Aziel?". The voice filled the room and seemed to shake the shadows. The room settled again but the slumber was waiting for a reply and the air seemed ready to respond if any word were uttered. Then, from the gloomy depths of the room came more words. Words that were as empty as the air. Insubstantial and light words that seemed to hang in the void. "No sir, everything is in order". The slow, deliberate, pronunciation could not give these words any body of importance. All was as it always had been and that was all that could be reported as it was at nightfall each day.

Day in, day out Aziel stood in that room watching from the small window by his shoulder and waiting for something to report. Never daring to speak unless addressed from the Chair and to Him conversation appeared to be a never indulged luxury and as sparse as the furniture in the room. The odd word, always a command, was all he uttered and occasionally -- and this was a thousand times worse -- a nod of the head or a glance in Aziel's direction was the only indication of this desire. It was as though He thought words wasted on Aziel; and although He had no-one else to talk to, He did not seem to desire anyone.

Words were of course wasted for the routine was adhered to so stringently that discussion had become superfluous. For as long as he could remember Aziel had come to this room at dawn to find Him already sitting in his Chair immediately opposite the door. As soon as he entered, he would extinguish the candles and take up his position by the window, in the far corner by the entrance. The Other always appeared soon afterwards and stood in the opposite corner. They had never spoken and at first Aziel had been pleased with what he regarded as his superior position with regard to the Other.

Because he had been there longer and arrived earlier for duty, Aziel had concluded that he must be senior to the Other. Every morning he extinguished and replaced the old candles with fresh ones for the evening. His responsibility for the candles and his charge over the Other had originally made him feel proud, for not many people worked for such a great man. Aziel reasoned that his master must be a great man to employ two servants in such a fashion. Who else but a great man would bother to afford two people to perform all the functions that He could as easily perform for Himself?

The work itself was easy. The master never expected his servants to exert themselves and Aziel had learnt to achieve his tasks with speed and efficiency. This entailed bringing the food, which was left outside the door at precisely the correct hour each day and placing it upon a small table beside His Chair. When He had finished, Aziel would remove the remains of the meal. Aziel had never seen who brought the food or how it was prepared and there was never a smell of cooking in the household. These facts helped to convince him of his position of second in the hierarchy for it was obvious that, whoever did the cooking, they were not allowed to enter the room. Over the years, the facts also brought about a feeling of fellowship in Aziel with regard to the Other. For although the Other was never allowed to approach the High Chair and stood in a windowless corner, he was obviously chosen to perform some function and was allowed to enter the presence of the Master.

So he stood quietly in the corner waiting for a word and allowing these feelings of smugness and self-satisfaction to grow. Like ugly worms, blind but irresistible, they slowly squirmed through his dark veins, eating his heart and his brain. Down the years Aziel stood staring at the High Chair, contemplating its occupant pondering on the High Chair and what immense task could keep Him in this immobility. The never changing sequence of events, the monotonous consistency of the room and the ever presence of the Master began to fill Aziel with revulsion. The vainglorious works of self-pride devoured all feeling of reverence for his Master and turned into hatred of Him and the immutable laws of this room. Aziel wanted to humiliate Him utterly; to see Him leave His Chair and get His own food, to check the window Himself, to walk round each candlestick at dusk and light His own candles. Better still, Aziel dreamed of following Him round, as He got the candle to light and moved on to the next branch he, Aziel, would blow out the newly-lit stand. The job would be never ending. Round and round Aziel, the All Powerful, would make him walk and still there would be no light. The darkness would creep across the floor from the dark corners of the room and out of the window into the cold world. The image of his tormented Master maintained Aziel through his endless days of routine and the darkness became his one desire. It took on all the characteristics of the evil worms that were over-running his body. The darkness would escape through the window and seep across the night sky, blotting out any vestige of light. The moon and the stars would be blanketed by the all-pervading dark and the Master would run around desperately trying to make light but every time He struck a match Aziel would be there to blow it out, causing the black smoke to rise and thicken the darkness. Thus a thick dark would cover the land so that when the morning came -- as he presumed it must -- the black would be strong enough to strangle even the sun's light and the Master would be too exhausted by his night of fruitless effort to do anything about the problem. Aziel pictured Him sinking to the floor beside the Chair, lost in a dreamless sleep, black and empty as the world into which only his own horrible echoing laughter could intrude. The idea became a longing not merely in the mind of Aziel but burning deep in his breast. An unfed want that became a need.

So these thoughts were constantly nagging in Aziel's mind as he waited, but he could not bring himself to make the decisive move necessary to overthrow his employer. He could not think why it should be impossible for him to make this move; his dream never included the necessary revolution; he had no knowledge of these affairs; he could not picture what would be needed for success until the importance of the Other became clear to him. In the past he had always imagined that the Other performed some menial task during the lighting of the candles, but this night he chanced to look back and see that the Other was not actually lighting any candles but was trimming them after they had been lit and cutting off old lumps of wax that had dripped on to the candlesticks. This was a revelation to Aziel: now he saw that if he were to take control not only must he overcome the Master but he must also overcome the Other, for he had a share in everything. The importance of the Other in the scheme increased Aziel's fellow feelings for they both had an interest in the candles and a very specialised job in their maintenance. A job, moreover, that he might not be prepared to forfeit. Now he realised the machine was complex. The social system within the room was set up in such a way that no-one could defeat the Master unless they knew how the machine worked but he, Aziel, had the key to the mechanism; and now all that was necessary was to find out how it fitted, and turn it.

For months, or even years, Aziel troubled himself with this problem. He watched the Other in his corner, hoping to see some form of rebellion in his movements but nothing gave any hint that this was possible. Finally, with his dream almost lost, in despair he saw that the only thing to do was to speak to the Other and to make him aware of their position. He would try to recruit the Other as an ally by showing him how they could have all the benefits of the Master without any of the tedium of their employment.

That night, after making his report, Aziel did not go straight home. Instead, after taking leave of the Master, he left the house and secreted himself in the shadow of the steps that led up to the great main doors. Eventually he heard the Other coming from the House. He walked round from the back of the house and passed the steps. Aziel hissed but the Other took no notice. A louder hiss but still no response from the seemingly oblivious Other. Aziel felt angry; it was obvious to him that he was going to have to catch hold of the Other if the plan was to be put into effect. Aziel let the Other get away from the house, following him at a short distance until he deemed it safe to approach him without the Master chancing to see them. He approached the Other from behind and tapped him on the sleeve. The Other turned slowly and Aziel could see at once that he was dealing with a very tired man. Aziel decided to go straight to his task.

"Hello", he said, with a false cheerfulness. "I thought it was you. I was just out for a walk when I saw you coming along. Just finished, eh? Bloody job, I can tell you it's getting me down, working for that old fool".

The treacherous words tripped off Aziel's tongue and gathered pace as he realised he was not being censured or contradicted by the Other.

"All He does" he continued, "is sit on that great seat of His all day. Never speaking, and not allowing anyone else to speak lest it disturbs His peace and quiet. What's he do that's so important? That's what I'd like to know! If he was writing a book or something you could understand but just sitting in silence all day!"

They were passing a small bar and Aziel changed tack.

"Do you realise that we've worked together for years and this is the first time we have spoken to each other? " This last statement was not strictly true for up to this point the conversation had been so one-sided that the Other had hardly had a chance to do more than mutter a few words. Aziel offered the tired man a drink and led him into the small dark bar which stank of stale tobacco and ale. As he ordered a couple of pints Aziel noticed that the Other liked the attention he was receiving and he realised that he was regarded as the senior member of the team. They stayed in the bar until late in the evening. Aziel paid for most of the drinks as they talked generally about their work and their employer. It soon became plain that the Other was as dissatisfied as Aziel about the conditions in which he worked but his plans were much less clear as to his bringing about a change. When Aziel was as sure as he could be about his man he asked if the Other had ever seen anybody else in the great room. Upon receiving a negative reply he said:

"So we are the only ones who know what goes on in there."

"I Suppose so" said the Other.

"Don't you see what this means?" said Aziel. "We can do what we want in there. We are the only people who can enter the room and the Master is too old to stop us doing anything. Tomorrow you don't have to trim the candles or stand in that boring corner. There's no reason why you shouldn't walk up and down. Put on heavy boots and stamp around. Knock Him off that silly seat. Only we will know and I will not say anything. We can have the Seat and He can stand in the corner. We can have his meals if we wish and I'll tell you that you will want them when you see what he eats. The food is beautifully prepared and always fresh, much better than what we live on with our rotten wages."

Aziel was carried along by his own fervour and the drink and he led the drunken and excited Other further and further into his plot until the revolution was all but accomplished by the time they left the bar that evening. Aziel had fed the discontent of the Other with his scheme until they were agreed that a change of regime was the only reasonable way out of the present boredom. What was needed was action and change and not this meaningless repetition of routine to satisfy the whims of some old man who appeared to do nothing but sit all day -- and probably all night -- in an uncomfortable High Chair. They were determined that tomorrow they would force the issue. They would free themselves of His constraints and then Aziel thought: "I'll show how a Master should behave".

All night Aziel could hardly sleep and when he did nod off his dreams were filled with orders of consequence, as he would have put it, and he saw great events occurring in the Room. The meals would not arrive at regular intervals, but all day a succession of the most delicious treats would be brought to the door. He would not sit there thinking all day. He would eat and drink and there would be music and girls, everything the heart could desire would he provided in excess. Of course, best of all, there would be the Master, now no more than a clown going round trying to light his candles.

At dawn Aziel was at work as usual but today he looked even more immaculately turned out than ever before; for today was to be an historic event. Today he was to become someone. He was going to make the choices. Ironically the Master did not even comment. As usual he had not noticed Aziel's attire and if he had perhaps he would have prevented the revolt. But perhaps not; who knows what goes on in the heads of old men. The Other arrived and Aziel glanced in his direction but saw nothing to inspire hope that the previous night's determination had not faded with the dawn. The Other stood quietly in his corner as before; he never moved nor even attempted to look out the window. The meals came and went as usual. The motes softly languished in the sunlight as it crossed the room and settled on the ledges already laden with dust. Time danced slowly with the shadows and Aziel came to think it was all hopeless as the dusk began to fall. It was obvious he had given the Other too much time to reconsider their plot. He should have forced the action and not allowed the Other to have a change of heart. He should not have allowed the Other to begin the revolt; that was his responsibility and he had failed; he had left it too long. These thoughts drummed in Aziel's brain until he felt he would rather die than give way. Even if there was no revolt he was not going to serve any longer, and with this decision he stepped forward.

"Anything wrong, Aziel" demanded the voice from the Chair.

"I'm off now", Aziel replied calmly and walked towards the doors, expecting at any moment that He would descend from the Chair but, unable to contemplate the consequences he would suffer, Aziel kept walking, fearing that his nerve would crack or his knees would give way, causing him to sink quivering to the floor. But as he reached the door he heard not the Master but the Other begging him to stop.

"Don't go, don't go yet". He turned and realised that the Other had also left his station and was capering round the room. "You've done it, don't you see you've done it. Stop in the room, let's carry out the plans we had last night. The revolution's won, He didn't even have anything to fight back with when you confronted Him like that".

Aziel stopped and realised it was true; for, although the Master was still sitting on the Chair he had not been able to prevent him leaving. Once he had conquered his own nerve he was a free man; he could act; it was simply a matter of overcoming a fear of a non-existent punishment. He turned back and walked boldly down the great room and up to the Chair. Although wearing the regulation slippers he deliberately placed his feet heavily to try and give more authority to his step. The Other followed closely at his heel. The Master never flinched -- but neither did he act and their eyes seemed held together by unseen cords. Neither blinked. At the foot of the Chair Aziel waited. The air was still once again, and within the silence the two opponents were held in a steely gaze.

For an age nothing moved. All the aeons of history were held trapped between the eyes of the Master and Aziel. It seemed that the very air must crack when, in a voice that summoned up every last effort of lungs and larynx Aziel issued his first command. If he was honest even Aziel would have to admit that his voice still sounded tiny in that great room. But this small action was his final treachery and he was very proud of it.

"Out! " he ordered.

The Master simply looked away. Aziel turned red with indignation and with all the veins in his temples swelling, he yelled this time. "Out!" But still the Master made no move to leave the Chair. Aziel saw his dreams crumbling again, for how can one revolt if even after the battle has been won the rulers do not respond to the demands and capitulate? He felt the Other nudging him. "Knock him off! Go on, knock him off". Aziel saw that it was the only answer; if the Master would not take orders he would have to be removed. He could not be allowed to sit there as though nothing had happened. Aziel leaped up to the Chair and grasped the Master with both hands and cast Him to the floor. Aziel broke into a mad laugh that echoed round the empty room and he slumped into the Chair. "Now you will serve me", he said as he remembered his dreams. "I am in control now. Go and light the candles". His mouth was drooling with the delight of it. It was even better than he had dreamt it would be. The Master would light the candles and the Other would blow them out while he, Aziel the All Powerful, would watch their manic dance. Then it was spoilt again.

"No", said the Master.

"He can't say that. He has to obey" reasoned Aziel, "for I am the Master in this room. I sit in the Chair." But what could Aziel do? The poor man had attained the seat of power and already there was a counter-revolution developing. "Light the candles" he ordered again, in a voice that now held something of a plea for Aziel knew that there was something happening that he could not understand.

Again the Master said "No" but added "I have no matches". Aziel fumbled in his pockets. It began to make sense of course. The former Master could not light the candles unless Aziel gave him the matches. He found the matches and tossed them to the Master who caught them effortlessly, moved forward and placed them beside the Chair.

Aziel saw that his revolution was in great danger of failing. Only one solution remained; the old Master had to die. It was obvious he could not be left around doing as he pleased. Once the decision was taken Aziel felt sorry for the old Master but he knew he had to establish his authority. And so with as much dignity as he could muster he issued the sentence of death. The old Master looked at him with a mixture of contempt and compassion and then said very slowly and deliberately: "That was the only choice left to you after all this. You don't know what you have taken on but I know you will wish me back again soon".

Aziel turned away and as if from nowhere the Other approached the Master carrying a two-handed sword which Aziel had certainly never seen in the room previously. The old Master nodded at the Other as though approving his action, knelt down and leaned forward. The Other raised the sword high above his head and with a great sweep which filled the room with wind and caused the curtains to flap and the hangings above the fireplace to fall into the hearth, he sliced the old Master just below the shoulder blades. The arms fell separate from the body; the old Master lay in four pieces among the settling dust. Aziel immediately turned to the Other; "You bloody fool, couldn't you even do that properly?" His face was grey and aged and the room sank into silence once again.

For three days nobody moved in the room. The body lay in four pieces at the foot of the Chair where Aziel sat staring vacantly into the air and the Other had retreated into the darkest corner immediately after the deed. The sword lay on the floor among the pieces of the old Master and the blood on and around it had gone hard and turned black. "This isn't what I wanted. This isn't it at all" thought Aziel and suddenly he dived from the Chair and had picked up the head. It was only then that he realised that the cut had made a bust like one of the immortal Caesars. He had meant to order the Other to remove the remains but discovered he was so filled with revulsion for a man who was capable to committing such an offence as to kill the Master who had protected, fed and clothed him that he had nothing to say. He could not determine if he was angry with the Other because of his own guilt or that of the Other; all he knew was that because of the guilt there was nothing to say. How could one say anything after such a crime? For those who had committed it were worse than nothing because they had created nothingness. with the Master gone they had no reason to continue and might just as well join Him who had been their source of life and had given direction to their hours. But Worse torment was to come to Aziel while he was engaged in this silent reproach of himself. He knew now that it was himself he was condemning. He saw that when he sentenced the Master he had ordered his own death and now in this great, empty room stood two useless beings unable even to communicate for they had nothing to say. Aziel had tried to give an order but discovered there was nothing he desired and he certainly could not think of enjoying the position he had so treacherously usurped. Even the blackness he had dreamed of, had lost its poignancy for what could be blacker and more desolate than himself? 'And after the Master had died what could be gained in chasing that hollow wretch, the Other around the room?

Now he sat at the foot of the chair, holding the bust of the old Master against his breast; tears streamed down his cheeks on to the lips of the old man. "If only there had been another way, another way" he kept repeating and stroking the beard on the old man's chin. Then he felt movement, the chin was alive and the eyes of the truncated head opened. Normally Aziel would have shrunk back with horror but this time he looked into those eyes and saw peace and laughter. Then with a wicked gaiety the head shook and said "Didn't I warn you that you'd want me back again? Ah, but you took no notice". Aziel wanted to interrupt, to beg forgiveness, to sing praises but the old man continued: "It's always the same and always has been. Each one who sits in that chair waits for the next one to come along and wonders how long it will be before he is forgiven for his presumption. We all want to make the act of freedom but how many can bear the responsibility of the free? So we act and find ourselves in tighter chains than before for now others rely on us. Once we could choose to act or not to act, not to enter this room even, but whosoever has this chair must act or the machine grinds to a halt. It is your job now; you can languish in this chair forever or you can keep the machine in order and hope for release."

Aziel began to understand the situation and looked up to see a new figure entering the room and taking up position where the Other had once stood. Searching the shadows he saw the Other now stood in his former place by the window. The horror overwhelmed him. "Oh, God! oh, my God! " he cried. "What have I done? How long will it take to undo this wrong?"

The Head nodded across at the Other. "As long as it takes him to forget. An age, or an age of ages, perhaps". with that, it slept again.

"Is it worth it, is it?" questioned Aziel. But no answer was ventured. Aziel placed the head back with the body and noticed the sword had been removed; he could not explain how. He ascended the Chair. He had to give the order, but could he? Was it worth the effort? And would his voice be heard in the immensity of this room?

The Voice
of
One Crying

a short story

THE VOICE OF ONE CRYING

Oh the lies that you tell yourself, or you do not even know what you say! 'Accept success, claim it, fight for it, but succeed'. Why do you do this, people, are you blind to the trap that you place around yourselves? Nobody warns you against this and only your greatest men see it — and you reject them. But you don't reject them for the truly Great Man has already rejected you. He has seen the secret of the universe, he knows the paths of understanding and he doesn't need your acclaim. He has all the success he wants in the knowledge of its worth.

See how you ignore the truth you hypocrites, you invented religion to give everyone the power to succeed, oh vain hope. The power to succeed, even your own inventions fail you. Religion is a hope not a method of success and when this failed you, you lied about religion. When you read in your bible how many of your heroes succeeded? Moses died before reaching the Promised Land and he is buried "ever against Bethper but no man knoweth of his sepulchre unto this day." Moses never tasted success, the milk and honey were not for him, oh would that we had learnt our lesson from him. But no we must build a society, develop a system, establish a ritual so that the successful man can boast of his success before the God he imagines ordained it. Before the God who gave him the power to murder, to rape, to plunder and call this success attributing it to some Divine Benevolence. His glorious victory.

> "Let the high praises of God be in their mouth, and a
> two-edged sword in their hand;
> To execute revenge upon the heathen, and punishments
> Upon the people,
> To bind their kings with chains, and their nobles with
> Fetters of iron;
> To execute upon them the judgement written: this
> Honour have all his saints, praise ye the Lord."

How cowardly can this man be; not even able to accept the consequences of the system he has developed, he then has to transfer the blame to the God he has invented in a form of praise and knowledge of his power.

How the prophets shame you, oh men of religion, men of society, believers in success. They had seen the Lord, they had true knowledge of God, and when they came to inform you they didn't wear royal robes, they didn't travel in golden chariots, or with hair richly adorned. The men of true knowledge owned no palaces, no horses, and had no retainers to run before them. They came dressed in rags, they wandered lonely in the wilderness, they ate the shit of cows and their hair was wild. These were the men of knowledge and see how the book testifies to the treatment they received from hands such as yours,

> "Woe to you, scribes or Pharisees, hypocrites! For you build the tombs of the prophets and adorn the monuments of the righteous, saying "If we had lived in the days of our fathers, we would not have taken part with them in shedding the blood of the prophets."

(Mat 23; 29-30)

So the book condemns those men of society, the men who wanted success couldn't allow the message of the prophets, the message which would destroy their reason of being, for without success these men were as nothing. Oh how the prophets realised this and in this lies their greatness. They accepted their fate without flinching and became like stone in the face of oppression.

In that condemnation, do you recognise yourself? It was written by one who knew, by one of those who followed the true prophet whose success was the lowest form of death, a crucifix, and whose final cry was an acknowledgement of his failure and his success —

"Eli, Eli, lama sadach — thani — My God, my God, why hast thou forsaken me." (Matt 28) "It is finished."

(John 19.30)

Even his choice of death reveals the nobility of this man for he chose the death scorned by those makers of the law, those men of society for had they not wrote —

"His body shall not remain all night upon the tree, but thou shalt in any wise bury him that day; (for he that is hanged is accursed of God;) that the land be not defiled, which the Lord thy God giveth thee for an inheritance."

These words show us the truth about these men. They are unable to stand alone. They refuse to be responsible for their actions. They are trapped by the values they create. See, even the body has to be nihilated — they dare not leave it to show how a man can reject them and stand alone. They profess concern for the land, don't be fooled, if a body can defile the land from the branches of a crucifix imagine what it can do from the depths of the earth and see again how the cowards shift responsibility for this action to the God of their invention.

So your religion is merely deception and the truly religious man doesn't reach for success. Therefore you create lies about the men of religion. Have you read about the four men who entered Paradise, Ben Azzie, Ben Zoma, Archer and R Akiba?

"R Akiba said to them, when you arrive at the stones of pure marble do not exclaim 'Water, Water'. Ben Azzie gazed and died; Ben Zoma gazed and became demented; Archer mutilated the shoots, R Akiba departed in peace."

(Talmud)

And we are told that Akiba was the true man, the man of religion, the success. But I say to you, read that story in true faith and see what it means. Surely the others have seen that 'the stones of pure marble' are not the absolute ground of being, there is no reason behind their existence and it is just as Akiba warns them a flowing, changing nothingness which is themselves. Thus the water is the soul which reflects the persona but which becomes blurred, the meaning lost once you try and touch it. It is this understanding that causes Ben Azzie's suicide and Ben Zoma's madness and leads Archer to find a new faith. Who is the true man? The true man is the one whose faith can be destroyed and he is able to change, virtually to recreate his ground of being and to live on despite his knowledge that he lives only for himself and for the project, which he establishes. But you praise Akiba, the man who departs in peace, and lives as though nothing has happened. While this nothingness is the very thing that has happened. He can not accept the failure of his mission, the failure which Akiba witnesses but ignores by recourse to bad faith. Do you think Akiba could have kept his position in society if he had understood what had happened? No, Akiba could not be a failure, he could not see that by failing he would succeed to put himself in a position of truth with regard to himself and his existence.

Let me show you how this was included in your own scriptures but you ignored it. We now see how the ordinary man can come by this knowledge which the rabbis learnt and the prophets held instinctively. Watch as Ammon trusts himself and realises in achieving his project the worthlessness of his aim. See what he attempts in the rape of his sister, Tamar.

> *"everything in the world is in a state of separation and dissolution; space always going out into more and more space; time passing, never having an end, sick with having no end. But being brother and sister, children of one father, they have the power to roll time back on itself, they can cram distance into their arms and hold it*

there, if only they dare to. No wonder the world would like to forbid them doing it; no wonder it would use all means to prevent them ....Yes, he and she, because they're brother and sister, born of one father, can together track back time and space to its source, to the original germ from which all things spring."

('The Rape of Tamar', Dan Jacobson)

But what are we told of him afterwards — "Then Amnon hated her exceedingly; so that the hatred wherewith he hated her was greater than the love wherewith he had loved her." Why, why, you should ask, why if she has led him back to the very ground of being? Open your eyes. Look, she had led him back, he has made the jump expecting to find the reason for his life. But what does he find — God, reason, logos, all these words of your philosophers. What are they but words? When he opens his eyes, Amnon finds nothing, he knows true knowledge, more than the prophets even. He is squarely faced with his own failure for he has failed through success whereas they succeed through failure.

What is this to me, you ask, all this happened a very long time ago and the world goes on. Why should I worry'? But I have already told you, and that strong Jew Matthew has also told you, you're a hypocrite. He saw what he believed in crucified and then he knew why he was living. Belief is a lie and the values of society are false precisely because they are social values. Therefore to be truly great you have to live outside society, living by values which you choose. Look at the society you place your confidence in with its ethic of success, where has it got you. Success depends on failure and as there is no way all of you can succeed the majority must fail with all the stigma that word attaches. Listen to my message — I'll write it in capitals — EMBRACE YOUR FAILURE, CHOOSE IT FREELY, BE JOYOUS IN IT. Now what can failure be but a success. Leave those lesser men to strive for success, it is for them that they can only live by the adulation of others. By your acceptance of failure you have succeeded. By asserting your Will on existence. You have transcended your failure by willing it and acknowledging the meaninglessness of their struggle. Let us leave this theme with the thought of the Psalmist – "Exalted be the God of Rock" (Ps 18) for this is what we must become. We must exist as the rock, exist for no reason but this one we impose, but we must be open to change as the rock constantly changes but remains itself without striving to be anything but what it is, existing in this moment.

"He sincerely seeks despair and failure when he is at his best."

(J.P. Sartre, St Genet)

www.ingramcontent.com/pod-product-compliance
Lightning Source LLC
Chambersburg PA
CBHW052129150426
42813CB00077B/2654